Sport with Trainer Tim

LEVEL 3

Written by: Maria Luisa Iturain
Series Editor: Melanie Williams

T0345650

Pearson Education Limited
Edinburgh Gate, Harlow,
Essex CM20 2JE, England
and Associated Companies throughout the world.

ISBN: 978-1-4082-8831-3

This edition first published by Pearson Education Ltd 2013
7 9 10 8
Text copyright © Pearson Education Ltd 2013

The moral rights of the author have been asserted
in accordance with the Copyright Designs and Patents Act 1988

Set in 17/21pt OT Fiendstar
Printed in China
SWTC/07

Acknowledgements
The publisher would like to thank the following for their kind permission to reproduce their photographs:
(Key: b-bottom; c-centre; l-left; r-right; t-top)

Alamy Images: Anne-Marie Palmer 13, Juergen Hasenkopf 21; **Corbis:** George Tiedemann 14-15;
DK Images: Susanna Price 10; **Fotolia.com:** Cherkas 23 (racket), Jacek Chabraszewski 11l, 23 (muscle),
ksena32@ukrpost.ua 6 (stopwatch), 23 (stopwatch), Paco Ayala 23 (cone); **FotoLibra:** Ray Lipscombe 17;
Getty Images: 3tc, 3tr, GLYN KIRK / AFP 18, Jupiterimages 9, NBAE 8, Popperfoto 3bl, 5, Time & Life Pictures
23t; **Photofusion Picture Library:** John Birdsall 22; **Press Association Images:** KEVORK DJANSEZIAN / AP 20,
MICHAEL PROBST / AP 4, THOMAS KIENZLE / AP 3tl; **Rex Features:** Most Wanted 3br;
Shutterstock.com: Kuzmin Andrey 12 (medal), 23 (medal); Studio 8: 6 (cone); **SuperStock:** Blend Images 16, Blue
Jean Images 11r, Image Source 19; **TopFoto:** 12
Cover images: Back: **Shutterstock.com:** Fotokostic

All other images © Pearson Education

In some instances we have been unable to trace the owners of copyright material,
and we would appreciate any information that would enable us to do so.

Illustrations: Gary Swift

All rights reserved; no part of this publication may be reproduced, stored in a retrieval system,
or transmitted in any form or by any means, electronic, mechanical, photocopying,
recording or otherwise, without the prior written permission of the Publishers.

For a complete list of the titles available in the Pearson English Kids Readers series, please go to
www.pearsonenglishkidsreaders.com. Alternatively, write to your local Pearson Education office or to
Pearson English Readers Marketing Department, Pearson Education, Edinburgh Gate, Harlow, Essex CM202JE, England.

Hello. My name is Tim. I am your trainer and I love sport.

We can have a lot of fun today.

I can help you learn about some different sports and some champions.

Then you can try some activities.

champion a very good sportsperson with a lot of medals

Athletics

Michael Johnson is a champion. He can run very fast.

Every day he trained and practised running.

He was a champion in a lot of different countries.

He was first in hundreds of races.

Where is he looking?
Can you see?
He is looking up.

balance

He uses his arms.
They help him to balance and to go faster.

He runs very fast.
He can run 10 metres in 1 second, yes ...
1 second!

Read and try

Now it is your turn to run.

Get a stopwatch and some cones.
Now you are ready for the race.

stopwatch

cone

Can you run 10 metres in 4 seconds?

Count the seconds and use a stopwatch.
You can start and finish the race with 2 cones.

Think about Michael Johnson and be a champion.

> **Remember!**
> Use your arms and look up.
> Your arms help you to run
> fast and to balance.

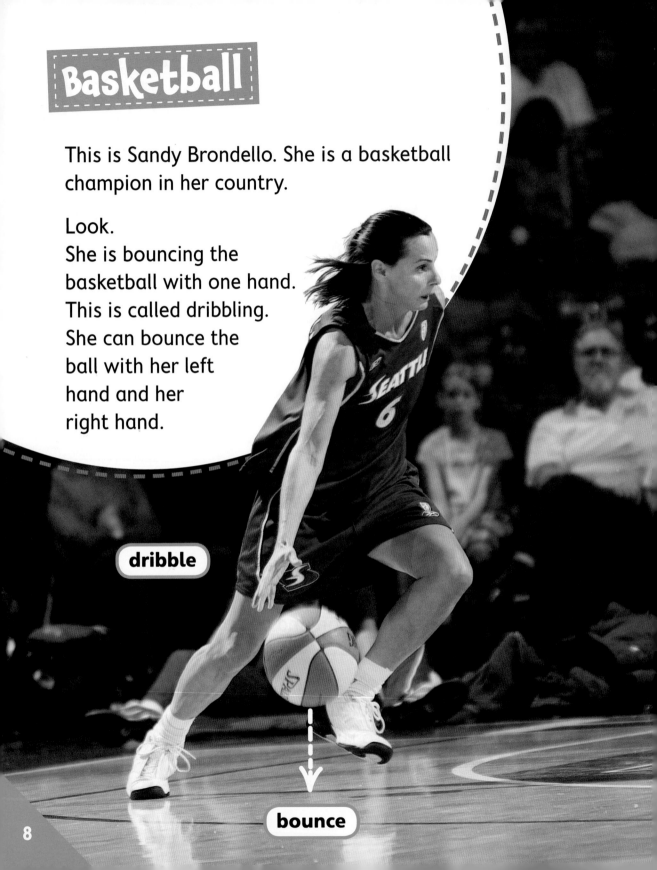

Basketball

This is Sandy Brondello. She is a basketball champion in her country.

Look.
She is bouncing the basketball with one hand.
This is called dribbling.
She can bounce the ball with her left hand and her right hand.

dribble

bounce

Read and try

Now it is your turn to dribble the basketball.
Can you bounce the ball with one hand?

Use the stopwatch.
Count the bounces in 30 seconds.

Think about Sandy Brondello.

> **Remember!**
> Dribble the ball with one hand.

Now play a game of basketball with a friend.

You have to dribble and control the basketball.
Your friend tries to get it.

Use the stopwatch.
Count 30 seconds.

After the game say 'Well played,' to your friend.

Now it is time to cool down.
Can you stretch your muscles?

Stretch the muscles in your arms.
Now, stretch the muscles in your legs.

The champions cool down after sport.

Remember!
Cool down and be
a champion.

stretch

muscle

Gymnastics

Olga Korbut is a champion. She is a gymnast.

She trained a lot and practised every day.
She wanted to be a champion.

She has got a lot of medals.

Look.
She is balancing on her hands.

medal

Read and try

Can you balance on one foot?
Can you balance on two hands?

Use the stopwatch.
Count the seconds.
Try and balance for 5 seconds on your hands.

Think about Olga Korbut and balance on two hands.

Football

This is Edson Pelé.
He is a champion and a great footballer.

He played many games for his country.
He has got many medals.

Look.
He is running with the ball.
This is called dribbling.
He controls the ball with his foot.

Can you see his arms?
They help him to balance.
He can run fast and control the ball.

He can dribble the ball with his
right foot and with his left foot.
He is a great footballer.

Read and try

Always warm up before you play football.

You can warm up and dribble the football.
Run in and out round the cones.

Use a stopwatch.
Count 30 seconds.

Remember!
It is important to warm up your muscles.

Are you ready to play football?
Have you got some cones and a football?

Think about Edson Pelé and be a champion.

> **Remember!**
> Use your right foot and your left foot.
> Control the ball.
> Use your arms. They balance you.

Tennis

This is Steffi Graf. She is a champion.

She trained every day and played many games.

Look.
She is looking at the tennis
ball. She is hitting
a forehand.

Can you look at
the ball and hit
a forehand?

forehand

Read and try

Use a tennis racket and a ball.
Hold the racket with a strong hand.
Watch the tennis ball bounce.

Can you hit 5 forehands
with your friend?

Remember!
Look at the ball.

racket

19

This is Andre Agassi.
He is a tennis champion.

He trained every day.
He first played tennis at the age of four.

Can you see?
He is hitting a backhand.
He is holding the tennis
racket with two hands.

backhand

Read and try

Can you play tennis with a friend?
Can you hit 5 backhands with
your friend?

After, you say 'Thank you,
well played,' to your friend.

Remember!
Look at the ball.
Hold the racket with
two strong hands.

Can you run fast?
Can you balance on your hands?
Can you dribble the football and basketball?
Can you hit a forehand and backhand?
Can you stretch after sport?

Yes, you can!
You can be a champion.

Activity page ❶

Before You Read

❶ Look at the pictures in the book.
Use the letters to make sport words.

a boatfoll
b thiacelts
c sinten
d tababelkls
e nagimysstc

❷ Match the words and pictures.

a stopwatch
b cone
c racket
d muscle
e medal

Activity page ❷

After You Read

1 **Read and write Yes (Y) or No (N)?**
   a Olga Korbut plays basketball.
   b Steffi Graf plays tennis.
   c Edson Pelé does gymnastics.
   d Michael Johnson does athletics.
   e Andre Agassi plays football.

2 **Match a – e with 1 – 5.**
   a Michael Johnson runs   **1** a forehand.
   b Sandy Brondello bounces   **2** very fast.
   c Olga Korbut balances   **3** the football.
   d Edson Pelé dribbles   **4** the basketball.
   e Steffi Graf hits   **5** on her hands.

3 **Which is your favourite sport?**
   Draw a picture of yourself.
   What sport are you playing?
   Write a sentence about what you can do.
   e.g. *I can play basketball.*